QUI

Tommy Steele was born
a popular recording artist a
has appeared in plays, operas, revues and pantomime throughout the world. As Arthur Kipps in *Half a Sixpence*, the musical version of an H.G. Wells novel, he starred on stage in London and New York and also in the major film. He has danced with Gene Kelly, filmed with Fred Astaire, and played Shakespeare with Sir Alex Guinness and Sir John Gielgud. His solo performance, *An Evening with Tommy Steele*, set a record for the longest running one-man show ever in London.

In addition to his world-wide success as an entertainer, he has received recognition as a composer, lyricist, painter, sculptor and writer. *Quincy* is his first book for children.

QUINCY

A Story for Children by

TOMMY STEELE

Illustrated by
Peter Wingham

Piccolo Books
in association with Heinemann

First published 1981 by William Heinemann Ltd
This Piccolo edition published 1983 by Pan Books Ltd,
Cavaye Place, London SW10 9PG
in association with William Heinemann Ltd

ISBN 0 330 28126 7
Printed and bound in Great Britain by
Cox & Wyman Ltd, Reading

For Emma

IT was six o'clock on the night before Christmas Eve in the toy shop. Bright lights blazed out from windows packed with toys as Christmas shoppers hurried home through snowy streets. Inside the store, the lights gradually went out on each floor as old Smithy slowly shuffled his way down the stairs. It had been a very busy day but now all was quiet.

As he reached the basement, Smithy shivered in the chill air. Hugging his coat more closely around him, he put on the dim light and went across to the shelf under the barred window. With a sigh he looked through the collection of broken toys until he found what he was searching for: a little boy doll called Quincy.

"There you are, Quincy," he said. "Come, I'll

take you over to my work table and see if there's anything I can do for you."

He picked up the little doll and went to sit down on a stool beside the table under the light. Carefully, he pushed back the sleeve of Quincy's jacket and studied the broken arm. Smithy was a big man and usually his face was cheerful and smiling, but now he frowned.

"It's no use, little Quincy," he said softly. "I'm sorry but I just can't help you or any of your toy friends. It's too late and there isn't time. I know I've neglected you for the last three weeks. You see, the new manager took me away from mending you and ordered me to do another job, and I've missed you all very much."

Quincy's bright painted eyes seemed to be looking at Smithy attentively and to understand all he said. He went on slowly, "I just don't know what I can do for you, unless . . ." He stopped for a moment and seemed to be thinking. "You see, the new manager doesn't want the broken toys to be mended at all. He says it isn't worth it. He calls you 'rejects' and he says that, tomorrow night after the store closes for Christmas, he's ordered the caretaker to . . . to throw you all into the furnace . . . and get rid of you."

In the stillness of the shadowy, dusty room,

there was a sound of sighing and Smithy felt something wet on the big thumb that was holding Quincy.

"Are you crying, Quincy, or is that my own tear? I'm sad enough to cry, even an old man like me, and I'd work all night if it would be of any use, but the manager says you won't be perfect

even after I've mended you. He wants only perfection . . . but he doesn't know the children as I do. Oh, dear, Quincy. If only . . ." He stopped speaking.

Smithy stood up stiffly and carried Quincy back to his place on the shelf among all the other damaged or broken toys. Tying his scarf tightly round his neck, he put out the light and went slowly up the stairs out into the bitter night.

Five long hours after Smithy had gone, the clock on the church tower outside struck twelve. With each stroke, strange things began to happen in the basement of the toy shop. The dark room was bathed in soft moonlight which came through the bars of the window. When the beams reached Quincy, he started to glow. Then, as if by magic, he moved his little fingers, he twitched his little nose, he blinked his little eyes. Suddenly, he was alive. He was no longer a toy but a real miniature boy. He examined himself slowly and he was rather pleased with what he saw. He looked round him at toys of every description huddled together on the shelves and in the corners. Quincy tried to attract their attention.

"Hey!" he said in a loud whisper. "Hey, you over there!"

When there was no reaction he gave a shout. "Hey! Anybody awake?"

As there was still no sound, he decided to get down off the shelf. Taking a deep breath, and feeling very brave, he jumped to the basement floor. Then, looking round with a defiant shrug of his little shoulders, he gave a piercing whistle. One by one, the other discarded toys came to life as the moonlight touched them; and they began

to chatter excitedly among themselves. All at once, a voice thundered over the noise.

"Order! Order, I say!"

The toys fell silent and out of the shadows swaggered a large teddy bear with stuffing sticking out of his body. He waited until there was complete silence. "Now you all know me, my friends, and you all know that I don't beat about the bush," said the teddy bear.

The other toys mumbled agreement.

"And I say that this isn't the time for singing and playing the fool. You heard what Smithy said. We're in terrible danger."

With a sharp "toot, toot", a small wooden train rolled into the centre of the room. "Teddy's right, folks," said Puffer. "These are hard times for us rejects."

Griselda, a rather tattered fairy with a broken wand, began to cry. "I don't want to be put on the fire and burnt," she sobbed.

"Cheer up, Griselda," Quincy said. "Let's enjoy ourselves and play while we can."

Now Griselda was even more distressed. "You haven't been here as long as the rest of us, Quincy," she said. "You don't understand. You don't even know why we've come to life."

"No," said Quincy. "I don't know anything.

Please won't somebody explain?"

At this all the toys started to argue amongst themselves. Suddenly there was a loud knocking noise. They all turned towards a big box from which came a muffled voice.

"If someone will kindly push my button, *I'll* tell him," said the voice.

Quincy, a little frightened now, walked up to the box and pushed a button on the front. With a loud crash, a Jack-in-the-Box sprang out in a flash of sparks. "Oh, my aching back," he grunted.

"It's because it's the night before Christmas Eve, you see, Quincy," said Jack. "On that one night of the year, as the moonlight floods in through the windows and touches each one of the toys in the store, we all come to life – just for a night. Then on the stroke of eight o'clock in the morning, when the shop opens, we all become toys again."

"I see," said Quincy thoughtfully. "So if we are to do anything to save ourselves, we must do it before eight tomorrow morning."

"But what can we do?" wailed Griselda.

All the toys fell silent.

"I know!" shouted Quincy. "I'll ask Santa Claus to help us!"

"Don't be silly, Quincy," said Teddy. "How could he?"

"Didn't you know that he grants a wish to all the children who come and sit on his lap?" said Quincy. "Now I'm a real boy, I'm sure he'll grant a wish to me. I'll ask him to save us!"

"But Santa Claus is right at the top of the store, in the Grotto on the third floor, and we're at the bottom," said Griselda. "You'll never get up there."

"I'm a boy, aren't I?" said Quincy. "I can climb the stairs like other boys can."

"It's a long way," said Teddy doubtfully.

"And there are terrible dangers," said Jack. "Once you're out of the Reject Department, you'll be on your own. All the other toys despise us rejects, and you won't have any friends to help you."

"You might meet the Robots," said Puffer.

"Or the Witch!" cried Griselda.

At the mention of the Witch all the toys shuddered.

"The Witch hates us," said Jack. "She'll do anything to get rid of us."

Quincy began to feel very small and very frightened.

"I . . . I think perhaps . . . well, perhaps I'd better not go. I . . . I just don't think . . . "

"Don't change your mind now, Quincy," begged Griselda. "You're the only one who can help us. In just a few hours we shall all become toys again and we'll never have another chance to save ourselves before we go into the fire. Please, Quincy . . . Oh please . . . and hurry. There isn't a moment to lose!"

At this, Quincy stood up very straight. He was trembling from head to foot, but he tried to be brave. Santa Claus was their only hope, and only he could save them. All the toys wished him well, each in its own way. Then before anyone could say another word, he turned and walked quickly towards the huge doors of the basement. Would he ever be able to open them? With a sigh of relief, he saw that Smithy had left them ajar.

Quincy walked through into the gloomy passage. Now he was all alone. The excited voices of the toys could no longer be heard. He looked up at the high walls on either side, and felt as though he was in a deep valley between mountains. The light filtering through was just enough to give him a huge shadow and, when he noticed this, his heart nearly stopped beating for a moment. Shaking a little, he spoke out loud into the silence. "Cor, you gave me a fright there, Shadow! I didn't know what you were. Well, I know you'll be with me from here on, all the long way."

Quincy started to feel his way further and further along the wall. "All we have to do is to find out how to get to the ground floor and then we're on our way. There, that's better, Shadow. Please keep close to me. I'll be needing company."

At the end of the passage was a gigantic spiral stairway leading to the ground floor. Each step was nearly as tall as Quincy.

"I'll just have to scramble up as best I can," thought Quincy. "But it will take hours! I'll never get to Santa Claus in time, if it's going to be like this all the way!"

But he gritted his teeth and, almost as if his shadow was pushing as well, heaved himself up to the top of the first step, then the next, and the next, until he reached the top. He sat down for a rest, panting but triumphant.

Ahead of him was a large sign that said:

Ground Floor – INDOOR GAMES

A door stood open and Quincy could see into a lighted room. He could hear the clicking of balls from a game of snooker, accompanied by music from a honkytonk piano that sounded jolly and friendly.

£2000

Quincy got up and walked into the room. There, bent over a snooker table, was a huge stuffed dummy. He wore spats, a sharp checked suit and a nifty bowler hat perched at a cheeky angle on top of his head. A cigar drooped from the corner of his mouth and he looked just like an old-fashioned gangster. Sitting at the piano in the corner was a kangaroo. Startled, the dummy and the kangaroo turned to look at Quincy, but the piano continued to play on its own. The kangaroo hastily flicked a switch and the mechanical piano ground to a halt.

"Excuse me," said Quincy politely, "but I wonder if I could come in?"

The gangster dummy smirked. "Our pleasure, dear boy. Perhaps an introduction is in order."

"My name's Quincy."

"Pleased to meet you. You have the honour to make the acquaintance of C.B. Cockerell O'Doodle," said the dummy. "My friends, creditors and members of the local constabulary call me Doodle . . . May I present my colleague Mr Kit, late of the Australian Outback and Up Front Brigade of Guards, philosopher, soothsayer, conversationalist, and chess master extraordinaire. Second to none in the art of fisticuffs and a rare delight at the gaming tables."

Doodle snapped his fingers. The kangaroo curled himself up into a makeshift ball and Doodle rolled him at top speed at a row of skittles. Bells rang and lights flashed as all the skittles fell at once. The kangaroo, shaking his aching head in the midst of the fallen skittles, bowed at Doodle.

"Well done, Kit," said Doodle. He turned and thrusting his face close to Quincy's, he said in a sneering voice, "Do you like gambling, lad?"

"What's gambling?" said Quincy.

Doodle stared in astonishment. "Do you mean to say you don't know?" he asked.

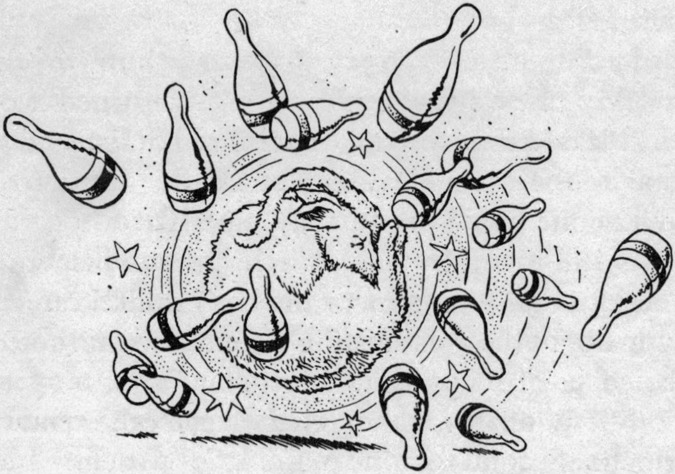

"No," said Quincy, abashed. "You see, I don't belong here. I'm on my way to see Santa Claus."

"On the way to see Santa Claus!" hooted Doodle. He burst out laughing. He couldn't seem to stop. At last he pulled himself together, put his hand on Quincy's shoulder and smiled his false smile, saying, "Fear not, dear Quincy, you are among friends."

"Oh really, am I?" Quincy was greatly relieved. "You mean I can count on you to show me the way to where Santa is?"

"You can count on me for help and guidance, dear fellow," said Doodle. "What are friends for, eh? Kit, a little soothing music for our friend."

Kit nodded. Quincy followed him to the piano and sat next to him, while he turned it on and played a tune. As Quincy and Kit listened to the music, Doodle crept stealthily away to a telephone booth and dialled quietly.

"Hello, is that the Witch?" he whispered. "Listen, you don't know me but I think I can tell you something interesting about a certain reject . . . if you're willing to pay for it."

The Witch's voice cackled on the other end of the line.

"It's a deal," said Doodle, chuckling to himself. He replaced the receiver quietly and ran back to Kit at the piano.

"Enough of this madness, Kit," he shouted, and picked Quincy up roughly by the scruff of the neck.

"Mr Doodle! Mr Kit! What is it? What's the matter?" Quincy cried.

"We're shut," said Doodle. "Closed . . . finished. Out to lunch, dinner, anything. Goodnight. Goodbye. Good luck. Good riddance!" With this, he threw Quincy out through the door, banged it shut, locked it and switched off the light.

Quincy found himself sitting on a hard floor back at the top of the spiral staircase. It was so dark now that he couldn't even see his shadow.

"Mr Doodle! Mr Kit!" he called. But there was no answer.

Poor Quincy didn't know what to do. He was very worried. It must be getting late. After a few moments he looked up and saw a faint glimmer of light from a window somewhere above him. He could just make out a staircase. He struggled to his feet and managed to climb slowly up the stairs until at the top he saw a lighted sign that said:

First Floor – MECHANICAL TOYS

To Quincy's relief the door again was open and he walked in between two high counters. Looking up, he could see all sorts of mechanical toys: monkeys, dogs, cats, elephants, ostriches, giraffes. As Quincy passed, they turned their heads with eerie mechanical clicks and peered down at him. It was frightening and he tried to hurry along but a menacing shadow crept up close behind his own shadow.

Quincy heard a slight noise. Glancing over his shoulder, he saw clawing hands reaching out towards him. The sound of a shrill cackle set him running as his shadow was torn from him. He stumbled behind one of the counters and tried to hide. He knew this must be the wicked Witch the reject toys had told him about and she had snatched away from him his only friend.

The watching mechanical toys whirred and buzzed and their heads clicked round and round as though they were very excited. All at once, they stopped and looked in the direction of some mechanical robots who were standing stiffly to attention. Silently a sinewy hand with long fingers and pointed nails slid out of the shadows and, one by one, set the robots in action. They started to move, heads turning and lights flashing with pulsating rhythm. Their arms were like crab claws jerking up and down. As they moved forward, these monsters gave off a high-pitched electronic signal. And . . . they were heading straight for Quincy's hiding place.

They came nearer and nearer in close formation as their electronic pulses reverberated with an ear-piercing screech. Terrified, Quincy turned tail and ran for his life. The robots glided after him while the other mechanical toys

watched eagerly. Then one of the robots fired a laser beam which shot from a big eye in the middle of its head. This barely missed Quincy and shattered a huge litter basket which burst into flames. Quincy dodged and dived desperately, as more laser beams shot out and tried to reach him. Closer and closer, the robots came. Now there was nowhere to go – his back against a high wall. On and on they came, shrieking as if they sensed victory. In the moving shadows he saw the sinewy hand of the Witch reach out towards a switch on a remote control panel. The panel was marked with one word: 'Exterminate'.

"No! No! Help, help, help!" Quincy cried.

At that moment a loud humming sound rose above the chaos. It was altogether different from the sound of the robots, louder, more dominant. Quincy was forgotten for the moment as the robots prepared themselves for an attack from the rear. Then gradually, they began to fuse, crackling and sparking from a series of short circuits. One by one the robots toppled onto their sides. Now they were nothing more than burnt-out mechanical dolls. With an angry screech the Witch took her hand from the switch and disappeared into the shadows, defeated. The hum came closer and out of the gloom appeared a top, a spinning, humming top. It circled round the smouldering mass of robots, made certain they were all out of action; and then, whirling round and round, it came up to Quincy where he was cowering against the wall.

Quincy stared at the top, which looked like a fat, jolly man.

"Hang on a minute, until I stop," it said. "Ah, that's better. I'm still a bit giddy. Oh, dear! It's all go, isn't it? Still, I heard your cry and I showed them who was the big noise around here, didn't I? Who are you, anyway?"

"I'm Quincy, and – oh – I'm so grateful for your help."

"Don't mention it, my boy. Quincy, eh? Well, dear me, I've never heard of you."

"I . . . I'm new here," Quincy said.

"Wherever do you come from?" When Quincy didn't immediately reply, the top spun round and round gently until he looked up. "I think I can guess. You've got a broken arm. You must be from the Reject Basement?"

Quincy nodded, a little embarrassed.

"That's nothing to be ashamed of," said the top. "It takes all kinds to make a toy shop, you know. Face up to the world. Be proud of yourself. You've got rights, you know."

"I'd like to believe that," said Quincy with a sigh. "I need all the help I can get."

"Then you've come to the right place," said the top. "If you want to get something done, there's nothing like starting at the top!"

For the first time, Quincy smiled just a little. "I'm trying to get to the third floor to see Santa Claus," he said.

"That's simple, son." As he spoke, the top was going round faster and faster with excitement. "You've got to climb two more floors before you get to the third floor where the Grotto is. Now go up these stairs." He pointed to a half-open door behind him. "That will take you to HOBBIES, GAMES AND PASTIMES, left past MODEL RAILWAYS, or is it right? No, forget that. Now, tell you what: get a car from SCALE MODELS and – where did you say you wanted to go?"

"Oh you do talk in circles!" Quincy laughed but he was worried. "I've only got until eight tomorrow morning and then I turn back into a toy again. I'll have to find my own way, thanks all the same."

"Anyway, you've got to get to the stairs through this door. Yes, yes, follow me." The top pushed through the door and moved off in a gliding fashion, turning occasionally. Then he stopped in front of another large door that was tightly shut.

"I can't open that door!" said Quincy in despair. "Whatever shall I do?"

"Hmm," said the top. "There must be a way. I know! We'll use building bricks."

There in the corner was a huge heap of bricks: As, Bs, Cs, Ds, Es – every letter in the alphabet. One by one, Quincy and the top piled them

together until they made a staircase so that Quincy could climb to the handle of the gigantic door which led to the stairs to the second floor. With a final wave of thanks to the top, Quincy struggled onto the doorhandle. He dangled there until it gradually lowered and opened the door. Then, taking a deep breath, he let himself drop down. At first he was a little stunned, but when he had recovered he saw the stairs and climbed them slowly. At the top he saw a sign that said:

Second Floor – TOY TOWN and BOOKS

He was glad to find that there was no door here but it seemed very quiet until suddenly the silence was broken by an eerie laugh. It was the Witch again. But Quincy felt braver now. He hoped that, after the defeat of the robots, she would not be ready to attack him so soon. All the same, he did wish that his friend the top was still with him. If only he could really see the Witch and not just hear her awful voice and see her great ugly claw-like hands and bony fingers!

Now it was quiet again, and Quincy called out bravely, "Has anyone here got the time, please?" And, as he spoke, the distant clock outside the church tower started to chime, and he counted seven slow strokes. Seven o'clock already! Quincy had no idea it was so late. Then, very gently, light came from nearby and he saw a beautiful painted sunrise, with a toy sun rising over a Toy Town which had a church on a hill, a school, a town hall, and rows of pretty dolls' houses. Gradually the Toy Town people began

MILK
JS3

to appear: housewives with husbands off to work, milkmen, newspaper boys, policemen, postmen, everyone you can imagine in any town anywhere. Quincy started to walk down the Toy Town street and wished his shadow was still close behind him. As he stopped by a lamp post, uncertain which way to go, he saw a beautiful rag doll.

"Hello," she said. "Who are you? It's nice to see someone new around here."

"I'm sorry, I can't stop," said Quincy. "I'm in a terrible rush. I've got something very important to do, and I've only got one hour left."

"Perhaps I can help," said the doll.

"I'm afraid you can't, though it's very kind of you. The only person who can help me is Santa Claus."

"Santa Claus? But why? Do you have a special wish?"

She looked so kind that Quincy decided to tell her everything. "My name's Quincy and, you see," he said, holding up his broken arm, "I'm one of many rejects. We've been waiting in the basement to be mended but now we're going to be burnt because the new manager only wants perfect toys to sell in the shop. If Santa Claus grants me a wish, I can ask him to save us all. But I've got to reach him by eight o'clock before we're all turned back into toys."

The rag doll sniffed as tears started to trickle down her face.

"Why are you crying?" said Quincy. "I'm the one who should be sad."

The rag doll took his arm. "Quincy, I'm beginning to lose my stuffing – just here." She held up a stuffed foot. "And they said yesterday I'd have to go down to Rejects."

"Then why don't you come with me?" said Quincy. "Santa Claus will save you too."

"Oh, can I, Quincy?" The rag doll's face

brightened. "I think I know the quickest way to find Santa."

"But the Witch is after me," said Quincy anxiously. "If she thinks you're helping me she'll try to get rid of you as well. We'll have to go carefully."

The rag doll tucked her hand tightly through Quincy's good arm and said seriously, "Quincy, my name is Rebecca, and I shall be your friend. Real friends stay together whatever the dangers. I know I can help you."

After that, they walked along arm in arm for a while until they passed a field where there was a scarecrow in an old soldier's uniform.

"Quick," said Rebecca. "Put that old uniform on. It will make a disguise so the Witch won't recognise you."

Quincy jumped over the fence into the field and scampered towards the scarecrow. He hastily put on the faded jacket, the busby hat, and the sword. "Well, what do you think?" he said, looking a little pleased with himself as he did up the last brass button.

"Oh Quincy," said Rebecca, "you do look so brave!"

They walked on, enjoying the sunshine. Now that Rebecca was with him Quincy didn't need to look for his shadow any more. Rounding the next corner, they saw a fort surrounded by a moat. The drawbridge fell, the flag rose, and a regiment of toy soldiers marched over the bridge in tight formation. Seeing Quincy, the Sergeant Major called out, "You there! Get fell in, Soldier." At this, he and several others came up to Quincy and pushed him into the ranks.

"I'm not a soldier!" cried Quincy. "Look, this is just an old uniform I got from a scarecrow. Leave me alone!"

But the soldiers paid no attention and poor Rebecca could only look on helplessly.

"Oh, oh, do take care," she cried.

"I'll try to. Don't be afraid. We'll find each other again," Quincy called back. He turned to the soldier on his right and said, "Where are we going?"

The soldier looked ahead all the time, his eyes never moving. "To the battle, or course," he said.

"What's a battle?" Quincy asked.

"That's where we fight the Foe, and get ourselves smithereened."

"What's smithereened?"

"It's the war game, mate," said the soldier.

The regiment marched into a great battlefield. The bugle sounded again, accompanied by fife and drums. Flags started to wave as the regiment broke into ranks and stood to attention. Quincy spoke from the corner of his mouth to his comrade. "What are we fighting for?"

"Don't ask me. I'm just a soldier," said the soldier.

As he spoke, the Foe, a great enemy army, appeared from behind a clump of trees.

A loud voice broke the peace with one word: "Fight!"

Cannons roared. Rifles and muskets were fired, reloaded and fired again. The smoke made it difficult to see the men who were falling on all sides.

"It's nearly our turn, mate! It's nearly our turn to be smithereened!" the soldier shouted excitedly.

Quincy, terribly alarmed, said, "I—I don't like this."

"You don't have to like it. You're a soldier and that's what you're here for, to get smithereened."

The battle was now much too close to Quincy for comfort. "But I don't understand why we

have to do it," he said.

"It's the Cause," said his comrade.

"What's the Cause?"

"Dunno," answered the soldier. "Ask the officers."

"Where are they?"

"Up there," said his comrade, pointing to the top of a flat hill where a group of men in officers' uniforms were sitting on life-size rocking horses, drinking tea.

"I'll go and talk to them," said Quincy.

"Don't go now," advised his comrade. "It's nearly our turn. You'll miss getting smithereened."

Since that was just what Quincy wanted to do, he made a dash for the hill but stopped at the bottom and glared up at the officers. "Hey, up there!" he shouted. "I've got a complaint!"

One officer, a podgy general with a very red face, spluttered into a tea cup and saucer. "What's that? What? What? What are you doing there? Get back into the battle. You . . . you . . . " he screamed down the hill at Quincy.

"No. No, thanks. I'll just stay here if you don't mind," Quincy shouted back.

"This hill is for officers only," roared the General.

"Well then, I'll be an officer," cried Quincy.

"Well, you can't. So there. You're not qualified to lead!"

"I'm not qualified to get smithereened either," said Quincy.

"You'll just have to be. It's orders. Otherwise, you'll be smithereened for desertion."

"Just a minute . . . just a minute," cried Quincy. "If I go back I'll get smithereened, and if I stay I'll get smithereened. That's not fair!"

"It doesn't have to be fair," yelled the General, nearly falling off his rocking horse. "It's the regulations. Now just be a good lad and get smithereened properly like the rest of them."

Quincy didn't know what to do. Perhaps the battle was best. He turned and hurried back through the smoke and noise and was greatly relieved to see that the fight seemed to be over. He stepped over the fallen men until he found his comrade lying stiff on the ground. Quincy looked down at him and felt very sad. The wounded soldiers reminded him of his own broken arm and his bruised and battered friends in the Reject Basement. They, too, would have a terrible fate if he failed in his mission for them.

The men on both sides who were still standing upright looked at him in amazement as he wandered through the battlefield. The officers on the hill stood up in their stirrups and shook their fists at Quincy. But he was in a dream, his mind was on his friends and he felt as though he could hear their voices. "Good old Quincy," Teddy was saying. "Take care, Quincy, we'll all be thinking of you." That was Griselda. "Brave old Quincy," Jack was saying, and Puffer called, "You've only got till eight o'clock, after that we'll be done for." "Done for," said Teddy. "Eight o'clock," said Griselda. "Done for," said Jack. "Eight o'clock," came the echo from Puffer.

Quincy, the voices echoing in his head, now hurried on until he came to a model railway station where the wounded soldiers were being taken back to hospital. A soldier came up to him with a cup of tea. "Like something warm?" he asked.

"No thank you, not just now."

"Something wrong?" asked the soldier.

"Everything," Quincy said. "I was just thinking – thinking what a failure I am."

"How so?"

"Oh, it's a long story," Quincy whispered,

almost to himself. "You see, I was given something important to do and now I'm afraid it's too late. I've got to reach Santa Claus by eight o'clock in the morning to save my friends, and I'll never get there in time."

"Nonsense, you're nearly there already!" said the soldier. "You're only a few minutes from the Fairy Book Mountain. Once you've climbed it, anybody will be able to tell you where to find old Santa Claus. His Grotto's just above them on the third floor. That's your way, over there. Good luck, mate. Tell him about us soldiers, won't you? If we get over our battle wounds, we'd make a great present for this time of year."

This was good news. Perhaps, after all, he would get to Santa in time, and Quincy felt his strength and courage return. If only he knew where Rebecca was! There was no time now to go back and look for her. He walked on at a determined pace and was making good progress when he heard someone crying. He tiptoed towards a clump of trees and there, to his great joy, he saw Rebecca sitting on a large toadstool.

"Oh Quincy," she cried, "I thought you were dead! And it was all my fault for telling you to disguise yourself as a soldier."

"Don't worry," Quincy reassured her. "It's

all worked out in the end. We've found each other again and I met a soldier who has put me on the right track. Santa Claus isn't far from here – just up one more floor. We have to find some mountains. If you still want to come with me, hurry. There's no time to lose." And he started to walk off again at a brisk pace.

"You really believe you can do it, don't you?" Rebecca said, running along beside him.

"I've got to keep trying in spite of everything," Quincy replied breathlessly. "If everything that's happened is the worst that can happen, what else could happen?"

"Stop a moment and take off that dangerous uniform," said Rebecca. When he had done this she said, laughing, "Come on, I'll race you!"

They began to run towards some books arranged in a great pile. For a moment, Quincy and Rebecca stood gazing up at the fluffy clouds that raced across the peak of the book mountain. Winds howled round it, and high flying eagles circled overhead.

"It's terribly high, isn't it?" said Rebecca.

"Well, mountains are there to be climbed," Quincy said. "Are you sure you want to come?"

"Oh yes," she said eagerly.

"Come on then," said Quincy.

Book, by book, by book, by book, they climbed, helping each other when they could. At last, after what seemed a very long time, they reached the summit, and there, standing on the topmost book, they saw below them a wonderful Fairy Book Land. Books of all shapes and sizes were lying about, their pages open showing giant cut-outs and pop-ups of fantastic fairy tale scenes. Quincy and Rebecca held hands tightly. They had never seen anything so beautiful before.

But time was running short, and they had to find Santa Claus.

They climbed down as fast as they could into Fairy Book Land and started to explore, looking for the way up to Santa Claus. Before long they came to a signpost. "Nursery Rhymes" said the arm that pointed north; "Poetry" was south; "Songs" was to the east, and "Adventure" to the west.

"Let's see the nursery rhymes," said Rebecca.

"No, let's go into adventure," said Quincy.

They had started to argue when a voice interrupted them, saying, "Read the notice, children."

They looked up and there, sitting on a high

library stool, was a large worm. He had a bald head with long white hair straggling down the sides. He wore a green eyeshade and perched on his tiny nose was a pair of spectacles with magnifying lenses that made his beady eyes seem like huge saucers. He was dressed in an outsize starched collar curled at the ends, with a flowing black kerchief tied in a big knot around his neck.

He had no arms, but his tail-end managed to hold a quill pen with which he pointed at a notice. Quincy read it out loud: "Quiet please. Bookworm at work."

"Oh dear," Rebecca said, "I'm sorry, we didn't realise there was anyone here."

The bookworm became rather testy. "That's all very well, young woman, but my concentration has gone. Now let me see . . . " He consulted a book open in front of him. "Once upon a time . . . Dear me, that does sound old-fashioned. Oh well, press on. Once upon a time there was a . . . was a little . . . Once upon a time there was a little dormouse."

"We won't be a minute, sir," said Quincy.

"A minute," said the bookworm, giving a sorrowful laugh. "Do you realise how precious a minute is to me?"

"Yes I do," said Quincy. "I haven't got many of them left myself."

"Are you in a hurry too?" asked the bookworm.

"A desperate hurry," answered Quincy.

"Ah, desperate . . . ah, that's a word. Do you see these?" He indicated his book and they saw that it was filled with nothing but blank pages.

"These," said the bookworm, pointing to the

pages, "have to be filled with fairy stories by Christmas Day."

"But that's tomorrow. Do they have to be new ones?" Quincy asked anxiously.

"Yes," said the bookworm. "Children learn the old ones so fast these days we can't keep up. I've written nine hundred and ninety-nine but I need a thousand and I just can't manage the last one." At this, the bookworm started to cry and said, between sobs, "I've tried all the possible variations – giants, pixies, piggies, flying elephants, . . . but I'm afraid my old brain is quite exhausted! You'll have to excuse me while I have another little cry."

Quincy thought for a moment. Then he said, "If I could help you with the last story, do you think you could help us? You see, I've got to get to Santa Claus and I don't know which way to go."

"Can you really tell me a story? What is it?" asked the bookworm excitedly.

Quincy said quickly, "It's a story about a reject, a little boy who wasn't good enough because of a broken arm and was going to be burnt away to nothing. He lived in the Reject Department with Teddy, Puffer the train, and a fairy called Griselda and . . . "

"Oh, stop, stop!" cried the bookworm. "That's too terrible. No one would ever believe it."

"But it's true," said Quincy and Rebecca both together.

The bookworm looked over his spectacles. "You're not *the* little boy, are you? A r-e-j-e-c-t?" He spelt the word out slowly.

Quincy nodded. The bookworm pointed the quill. "Dear, dear. Well, I think I can manage the rest of the story myself. I do thank you but you'd better hurry along: past *Treasure Island*, left at *The House That Jack Built*, and then just follow the magic mirrors. You can't miss the way up to Santa's Grotto, right at the top, up one more flight of stairs."

"Thank you," said Quincy. But the bookworm couldn't speak. His tears were falling onto the pages as he began to write.

"Cheer up, Bookworm," Quincy called to him as they started to run off. "I think we may all have a happy ending."

Rebecca suddenly grasped Quincy's arm. "Look, there are the magic mirrors," she said.

"Oh, do come on!" said Quincy. "We haven't time to stand and stare."

"Stop, Quincy, please!" begged Rebecca. "Look in the mirror!"

Quincy looked where she pointed and froze in

his tracks. The hideous face of the Witch stared out from the mirror. There was a clap of thunder and a flash of lightning; and through it all they could hear the dreadful cackling laughter. "Now you can see me," she cried. "I am old, old, and ugly, but I'll get you yet!" As she spoke the dreadful laughter faded away in a final clap of thunder, and at the same moment Quincy and Rebecca felt something raining down from above.

It was silver and gold tinsel pouring down in such torrents that they were soon trapped in a

jungle of Christmas decorations. They could not move, or see, but they heard a bright breezy voice say, "It's a long road that has no turning."

Quincy and Rebecca could just see a Christmas cracker, a jolly shining Christmas cracker with a face peering out at them from the piles of tinsel and wrappings.

"Hello, hello," said the cracker. "How did you like my motto? Now, now, what have we got here? I say, what gloomy faces on Christmas Eve!"

"Oh, go away," cried Quincy in despair.

"Don't be like that," said the cracker. "It's Christmas time. I'm jolly Jim Cracker. Here, have another motto."

"No, no thanks," said Quincy, trying to disentangle his feet.

"Pity, it's a good one." He read it. "A stitch in time is worth two in the bush." The cracker folded up with laughter. "Oh, come on, you've got to get into the party spirit. Here, have a paper hat." He stuck a paper hat roughly onto Rebecca's head. "Now, that's better. How about one of Jolly Jim's jokes? Crackers' jokes always go with a bang. Get it? Bang! Oh, you didn't get it, did you? What's wrong with you?" He suddenly looked serious. "You're in trouble, aren't you? What's the matter? You just tell Uncle Jim."

"We've got to get to Santa Claus by eight o'clock," said Quincy. "And now we've got ourselves stuck here. We're trapped."

"Ah, that's no problem at all. It stands to reason, if you can get yourselves into the tinsel forest, you can get yourselves out. Now can't you?"

"Oh, oh, please do help us out of here!"

"In a jiffy, old son, but I've got to get a genuine laugh out of you first. Nobody's going to say that Jolly Jim Cracker failed in his job."

"All right. All right. Ha, ha." Quincy and Rebecca tried to laugh together.

"Come on," urged Jolly Jim. "You've got to do better that that! I'll tell you what: you tell me a joke. Go on, tell me a joke and if you can make me laugh, I'll see if I can help you. How's that?"

"But I've only got a few minutes left," said Quincy desperately. "I've got to get to Santa Claus's Grotto. It's a matter of life or . . . or burning."

"That's not funny at all," said the cracker. "Hey, that's the first time in my life I've ever said that! No, it certainly isn't funny, but I'll help you anyway. Come on, I'll clear a path for you so you can get to the lift. That's the quickest way up to the third floor."

As the cracker rolled over and over, the tinsel fell away, and Quincy and Rebecca followed Jolly Jim to the lift gates.

"But I can't reach the starting button and the lift's down below," said Quincy.

"That's easy," said the cracker. He pointed to the pulley cable dangling down the middle of the shaft. "Climb up the cable to the light at the top and you'll be in Santa's Grotto. Rebecca will have to go up by the stairs, although it'll be much slower."

Quincy was terrified. How could he possibly climb the cable with only one arm? Gritting his teeth, he took a death-defying leap into the darkness and gasped with relief as he caught hold of the cable with his good hand. It swayed a little but he held on with his knees and gradually it steadied. Now he could look up to see the welcoming light of Santa's Grotto shining through the lift door above. He had scarcely begun his climb before he heard a creaking, whirring noise which was getting louder by the second. Someone had started the lift! It was coming up under him, floor by floor, nearer and nearer.

This must be the Witch's work, a last desperate attempt to get rid of him before he reached

the safety of Santa's Grotto. How thankful he was that Rebecca had taken the long route. The shrill voice of the Witch echoed up the lift shaft, getting louder and harsher as the car made its rapid progress towards Quincy, dangling dangerously on the cable.

"Foolish boy," screamed the mocking voice, "you have only a few seconds left. Did you think I would let you and your little reject friends live happily ever after? How they mocked me because no child wanted me. Now it's my turn to laugh, as one by one they're burnt in the flames of the furnace," she cackled hideously.

Quincy lost all hope, but suddenly his mind cleared and he thought, "Why, if the lift comes up under me, I can drop onto its roof and ride up to the next floor." No sooner had he realised this than he bravely let go of the cable and dropped down onto the top of the lift which was now just below him.

Clank! Clank! Up it came and stopped with a jerk. Quincy crawled to the edge and peered over as the tall ungainly figure of the Witch walked out of the lift. She was making curious sounds but her movements were slow and clumsy.

"Why, she's only a toy witch who came to life just as I did," Quincy thought. Her arms and legs had become almost rigid as she tried to strut across the Grotto and reach her broomstick standing in the corner. "She's just made it,"

Quincy thought, and then he began to feel stiff himself.

"Oh, I must hurry, hurry," he cried out loud.

He managed to get down from the roof of the lift, half clinging to the side of the car, and ran stiffly towards Santa's great chair in the very centre of the beautiful green Grotto. Then he looked up.

The chair was empty!

At that very moment, the clock outside began

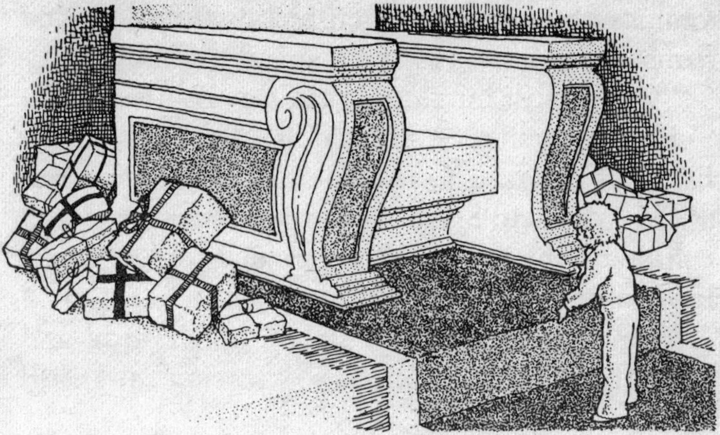

to strike slowly: one . . . two . . . three . . . four . . . five . . . six . . . seven . . . EIGHT!

Quincy was a toy again, standing in despair at the foot of Santa's empty chair. He had lost. He could feel his heart beating more and more slowly, and he could move nothing, not even a finger or an eyelid. Within a few seconds he was almost a toy again.

Sunlight suddenly streamed through a window and lit up the Grotto and the golden chair. Everything was as Quincy had imagined it would be. There was holly and ivy, there were Christmas trees laden with gold and silver decorations, there was a snowy carpet with red berries spelling WELCOME. And, yes, there in one dark corner was the hideous witch astride her broomstick – just a great ugly toy!

"Why, what's this?" said a gentle voice. "Look at your poor broken arm."

It was Santa Claus himself, looking down at the little boy doll. Under the pointed red cap and behind the flowing white beard, Quincy saw a kind face with twinkling eyes.

Santa Claus carefully picked up the doll and

held it lovingly as he climbed into his great chair, saying, "I know all about you and your sad friends, Quincy, and I also know all the toys come to life the night before Christmas Eve. I don't know how you did it but I think you must have come here all by yourself to ask me to grant a wish. Don't worry, I can certainly help you, and I won't let you or your friends be destroyed."

Then he stopped speaking as a small boy

appeared in the doorway. He was a serious child and he just stared in the direction of Santa, whose chubby arms now invited the boy to his lap. "What's your name?" he asked.

"David," said the boy, settling on Santa's knee.

"And what would you like for Christmas?"

The boy thought seriously. Suddenly he caught sight of brave, battered Quincy in Santa's hand.

"That doll," he said. "Oh, that's just what I wanted."

"His name is Quincy," said Santa.

Just then, a little girl came slowly into the room. She was carrying the rag doll tightly in her arms. "Look, look, David. Look, Santa, what I found lying on the floor just outside the door. She's got a poor hurt foot."

"Why, that's Rebecca. I wonder how she got there!" said Santa. "Climb up on my lap, little girl, there's room for you as well as David. You know each other, don't you?"

"Oh, yes, he's my brother." "And she's my sister, Mary." They both spoke at once.

Holding the two children in his lap, Santa said, "Is your Mummy or Daddy here?"

"No," David said, "we came with our teacher

Mrs Jones and the whole class – for a special treat. We haven't any money to buy toys but we came very early before the crowds so we could look around and . . . and . . . to see you, Santa Claus!"

"We rushed on ahead so we could be here first, but the others are coming up the stairs already," said Mary.

As she spoke, a smiling young woman came, followed by a clamouring crowd of small boys and girls.

Santa held up his hand and called to the teacher above the noise, and she came to his chair and leant over so that he could whisper to her. She smiled, Santa smiled, and they both clapped their hands. When the children were quiet, Mrs Jones said, "Santa's given us a wonderful surprise. To find it, we must go down the stairs quickly and quietly before anyone else comes. Follow me!"

They all filed out and David and Mary went after them with Quincy and Rebecca.

"Santa says we can keep them," David whispered excitedly.

"Yes, I know," Mary answered. "And he told me that they were going to be burned up tonight because they were rejects." She looked down at the rag doll. "I can be a nurse and mend your foot."

"And Daddy can mend Quincy's arm," David said happily.

"Yes. Oh, yes."

Now they were following Mrs Jones and the others into the dark basement. As she switched on the light the children cried out with excitement.

"Wait! Wait!" Mrs Jones called. "Santa says you can each have a toy of your own to take home. You see, they are broken, and were going to be thrown into the furnace tonight to be burned up, but you can save them. He says to take them all – every one, and if there are too many, you can give them to your brothers and sisters. Santa says they are all for you."

The children, screaming with delight, rushed about in the dim basement and fell on the toys. Teddy, Griselda, Puffer, Jack and every one of the toys soon had a boy or girl to love them. Every single toy was saved!

Mrs Jones clapped her hands again. "Come now," she said. "We must hurry back to the Grotto to thank Santa Claus for our wonderful Christmas presents!"

The children dashed up the four flights of

stairs laughing and chattering. Santa was sitting where they had left him in his big chair. He was smiling a very wide smile.

"Thank you Santa Claus, thank you!" cried all the children.

At this Santa raised his hand and beckoned to David who came to stand beside the chair. He was still tightly clutching Quincy.

Then Santa said, holding Quincy up for all to see, "It is this doll, Quincy, who has made this a Happy Christmas for you and for himself and all

his toy friends. He has been very brave, and perhaps some day he will tell you just how he did it. Let's give him a big cheer!"

The whole toy shop shook when together

they cried: "*Three cheers for Quincy.*" And then, "*Three cheers for Santa Claus!*"

Everyone was so happy that they didn't notice a tiny tear creeping out of Quincy's eye. But it wasn't a sad tear – it just meant he was the happiest person there.

Piccolo fiction you will enjoy

Emma in Love	Honor Arundel	60p
The Keyword and Other Mysteries	Isaac Asimov	90p
Are you There, God? It's Me, Margaret		£1.00p
Blubber		95p
Iggie's House		£1.00p
Otherwise Known as Sheila the Great	Judy Blume	£1.00p
Superfudge		£1.00p
Tales of a Fourth Grade Nothing		£1.00p
The Treasure of Dubarry Castle	Lindsay Brown	95p
The Secret of the Silver Lockets		£1.25p
Dolphin Island	Arthur C. Clarke	£1.25p
The String Family	Patricia Cleveland-Peck	95p
The String Family in Summer		95p
The Little Prince	Antoine de Saint Exupéry	95p
The Horses of Follyfoot	Monica Dickens	50p
Spring Comes to World's End		35p
Stranger at Follyfoot		60p
The Great Ghost Rescue	Eva Ibbotson	95p
Which Witch?		£1.25p
The Mouse that Roared	Ray Jones	90p